GETTING TO KNOW THE WORLD'S GREATEST COMPOSERS

IGOR
STRAVINSKY

WRITTEN AND ILLUSTRATED BY MIKE VENEZIA

CONSULTANT

DONALD FREUND, PROFESSOR OF COMPOSITION, INDIANA UNIVERSITY SCHOOL OF MUSIC

CHILDREN'S PRESS®
A DIVISION OF GROLIER PUBLISHING
NEW YORK LONDON HONG KONG SYDNEY
DANBURY, CONNECTICUT

Picture Acknowledgments
Music on the cover and title page, Stock Montage, Inc.; 3, Study of Igor Stravinsky by J-E Blanche, 1913, Musee des Beaux Arts, Rouen, Giraudon/Art Resource, NY; 4, Set design for *The Nightingale* by Natalya Gontcharova, Victoria & Albert Museum, London/Art Resource, NY; 5, Stage design by Alexandre Benois for *Petrushka,* Private Collection, Art Resource, NY; 8, Hulton Deutsch Collection Limited, London; 10, Igor Stravinsky Collection, Paul Sacher Stiftung, Basel, Switzerland; 14 (Rimsky-Korsakov, Cui, Borodin, & Mussorgsky), The Bettmann Archive; 14 (Balakirev), New York Public Library Picture Collection; 15, Sovfoto/ Eastfoto; 17, The Metropolitan Museum of Art, Bequest of Lizzie P. Bliss, 1931. (31.67.11); 19, The Bettmann Archive; 20, Leon Bakst, Sketch for the costume of Madame Karsavine from Diaghilev's production of The Firebird, Bibliotheque de l'Arsenal, Paris, France, Giraudon/Art Resource, NY; 21, Design of the curtain for *The Firebird,* Pavel, Kusnezov, Museo Statale Russo, St. Petersburg, Scala/ Art Resource, NY; 23, The Bettmann Archive; 25, © Collection Viollet, Paris; 27, 29, The Bettmann Archive; 30, Walt Disney (courtesy The Kobal Collection); 31, The Bettmann Archive; 32, Hulton Deutsch Collection Limited, London

Project Editor: Shari Joffe
Design: Steve Marton

Library of Congress Cataloging–in–Publication Data

Venezia, Mike.
    Igor Stravinsky / written and illustrated by Mike Venezia.
        p. cm.—(Getting to know the world's greatest composers)
    Summary: The life story of the Russian composer known for
    his musical innovations.
    ISBN 0-516-20054-2 (lib. bdg.) — ISBN 0-516-26076-6 (pbk.)
    1. Stravinsky, Igor, 1882-1971—Juvenile literature.
    2. Composers—Biography—Juvenile literature.
    [1. Stravinsky, Igor, 1882-1971.   2. Composers.]
    I. Title. II. Series: Venezia, Mike. Getting to know the world's
    greatest composers.
    ML3930.S86V46   1996
    780` .92—dc20

                                    96-13312
                                       CIP
                                     AC MN

A portrait of Igor Stravinsky in 1913

Igor Stravinsky was born in the Russian seaside town of Lomonosov in 1882. The exciting new rhythmic sounds he invented changed the way people thought about music forever.

Perhaps Igor Stravinsky's best-known musical pieces are the ones he wrote early on, when he was just starting out as a serious composer. Igor composed *The Firebird, Petrushka,* and *The Rite of Spring* between 1910 and 1913 for a new Russian ballet company.

A set design for *The Nightingale,* one of Stravinsky's earliest ballets

A set design for the ballet *Petrushka*

The Firebird is about a Russian fairy tale. *Petrushka* is a folktale, and *The Rite of Spring* is about an ancient and frightening Russian ceremony. Igor had a great gift. He was able to write music that went along perfectly with dancing and helped tell a story with sound.

Igor Stravinsky loved fairy tales and folk music. One of his first memories of music was when he was only about three years old. He was at a fair in the Russian countryside where the Stravinsky family often spent their summers.

There Igor saw a gigantic, bearded folk musician sitting on a tree stump. He was singing, clicking his tongue, and making loud armpit noises. Igor couldn't wait to get home and try making these noises himself.

When summer was over, the Stravinskys moved back to their apartment in the busy city of St. Petersburg, Russia. Years later, when Igor was composing music, he often remembered the sounds of St. Petersburg. Sounds that seemed ordinary to most people had a special meaning to him.

Igor never forgot the clear echo of horses hooves and the clanking of iron-rimmed wagon wheels on the cobblestone streets. He loved the bright clanging of church bells and the mechanical sounds coming from machine shops. All these things gave him lots of ideas for music later on.

The main street of St. Petersburg during Stravinsky's time

Igor Stravinsky grew up in a very musical family. His father was an important opera singer with the St. Petersburg opera, and his mother was an excellent pianist. Igor and his brothers often went to the opera while they were growing up. They heard their father's beautiful voice as he performed in the major operas of the day.

Igor's parents, Feodor and Anna Stravinsky, in 1896

One of Igor's most exciting memories came
during an intermission of one of these operas.
He saw his greatest music hero, composer
Peter Tchaikovsky. Igor saw Tchaikovsky for
only a split second, from far across the room,
but he never forgot that moment. It was the
only time Igor ever saw the great composer.
Peter Tchaikovsky died just a few weeks later.

Even though Igor Stravinsky came from a musical family, his parents didn't really encourage him to study music. They agreed to let him take piano lessons when he was nine years old, but they wanted him to become a lawyer someday.

Igor loved playing the piano more than anything. He learned quickly, and started to make up his own music. After he graduated from high school, Igor entered the University of St. Petersburg to study law.

Igor found studying law boring, and didn't do very well with his grades. He spent most of his time thinking about music. Things worked out though, because Igor became friends with a student named Vladimir Rimsky-Korsakov. Vladimir happened to be the son of one of Russia's greatest composers, Nikolay Rimsky-Korsakov!

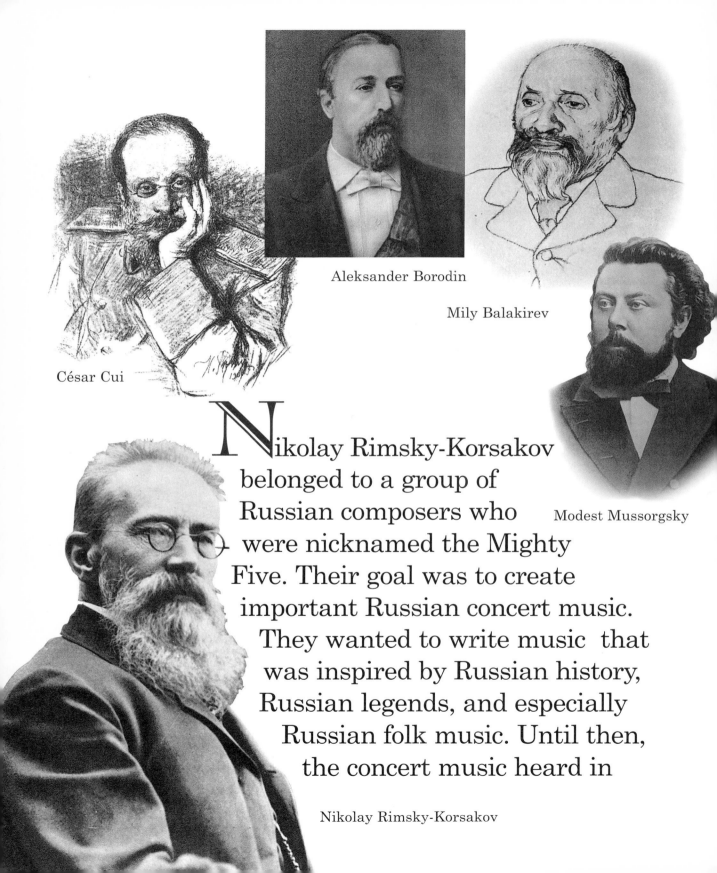

Aleksander Borodin

Mily Balakirev

César Cui

Modest Mussorgsky

Nikolay Rimsky-Korsakov belonged to a group of Russian composers who were nicknamed the Mighty Five. Their goal was to create important Russian concert music. They wanted to write music that was inspired by Russian history, Russian legends, and especially Russian folk music. Until then, the concert music heard in

Nikolay Rimsky-Korsakov

An illustration showing Russian folk dancing

Russia was written mostly by composers from other countries like France, Germany, Austria, and Italy.

Igor Stravinsky was introduced to Rimsky-Korsakov by his school friend. The great composer advised Igor to keep studying music. Soon after this, Igor's father died. Igor decided to forget about becoming a lawyer, and put all his efforts into becoming a serious composer.

Rimsky-Korsakov agreed to teach Igor.
He worked patiently with his new student,
and Igor learned all he could from his great
teacher. Igor studied the works of other
composers, too. One of his favorites was the
modern French composer Claude Debussy.

Debussy broke a lot of the music rules that
people had followed for a long time. He was
able to suggest feelings with his music.
He blended fuzzy bits and pieces of different
melodies together to give an impression of
dreamy images of nature. His music might
suggest billowy, drifting clouds; a moonlit
countryside; or the power and beauty of
the ocean. It's kind of the way the French
impressionist artists suggested their images,
only they used paint and color instead of
musical sounds.

The Manneporte, near Etretat, an 1886
painting by French impressionist artist
Claude Monet

When Igor Stravinsky started composing his own music, he often borrowed ideas from Debussy, Rimsky-Korsakov, Tchaikovsky, and other composers. When Igor was 26 years old, one of his first compositions, *Fireworks,* was performed in St. Petersburg.

It was an important day for Igor. In the audience was a man who enjoyed Igor's music so much that he wanted to hire him as a composer for an exciting new ballet company. Sergey Diaghilev was gathering up the best Russian dancers, choreographers, set and costume designers, and composers he could find. Diaghilev planned to take his ballet company to Paris, France, to show the world how great Russian music and dancing could be.

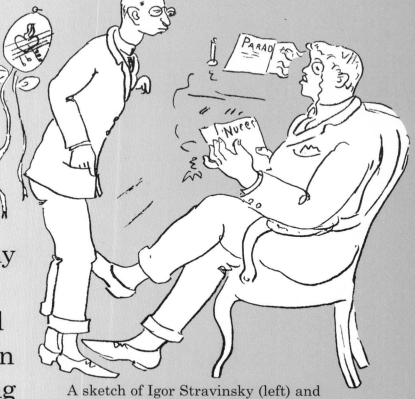

A sketch of Igor Stravinsky (left) and Sergey Diaghilev (right) discussing some music

Igor was thrilled to be asked to join the Russian ballet company. By this time, he was married and the father of two children, and he really needed the job.

After composing a couple of smaller pieces, Igor was asked to write music for a well-known fairy tale called "The Firebird." Igor loved the mystical story. He worked hard to make music that would fit the characters—the brave prince, the wicked wizard, and the magical firebird.

In his first important composition, Igor did everything he set out to do.

Sketches of a costume design (opposite page) and the curtain design (above) for the first production of *The Firebird*

His striking music, along with the beautiful costumes, set designs, and super-creative dancing, amazed everyone who saw *The Firebird* ballet.

When the ballerina playing the firebird first appeared, she did a series of gigantic leaps right across the stage! When you hear the music for that part, called "Firebird's Dance," it's easy to imagine a magical firebird whirling and sparkling and blazing across the sky. Igor Stravinsky created many dazzling music sounds that had never been heard before.

The Firebird was such a big hit that it turned Igor Stravinsky into a star composer overnight! Right away, he began working on his next ballet, *Petrushka*. It was about three puppets—a ballerina, a soldier, and Petrushka the clown—and an evil magician who was able to control the puppets so that they seemed to be alive. Many people feel that of all Stravinsky's ballets, this one does the best job of telling a story with musical sound.

Stravinsky with the world-famous Russian ballet dancer Vaslav Nijinsky, shown here dressed as the character Petrushka

$\mathbb{L}$ike *The Firebird, Petrushka* was a big hit, but Stravinsky's next ballet caused some problems. Igor began writing music for *The Rite of Spring*—a musical piece based on an idea he had. It's about a prehistoric tribal ceremony. Igor filled his music with energy and powerful rhythms.

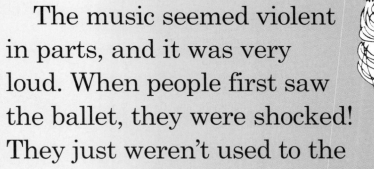

The music seemed violent in parts, and it was very loud. When people first saw the ballet, they were shocked! They just weren't used to the unexpected new sounds or the explosive dancing. The audience didn't know whether to laugh at the ballet or get angry. A riot broke out, and Igor was very upset. The following week, he became ill with a fever and had to take a long rest.

In time, *The Rite of Spring* became one of the most important musical pieces of the 20th century. Eventually, people found something in its wild, beating sounds that touched them deeply.

Sketches showing some of the movements of the dancers in *The Rite of Spring*

$\mathcal{S}$oon after Igor Stravinsky finished *The Rite of Spring,* World War I started. It was a rough time for Igor. During the war there was very little money to spend putting on ballets or concerts. Not only that, but both Igor and his wife had some serious medical problems. Igor decided to live in Switzerland, where his family could be close to the best medical centers.

The Stravinskys had four children now. They all had to stay in a crowded hotel room for a while, and Igor had a terrible time concentrating. He could compose music only if he were sure no one could hear him.

Fortunately, a generous music dealer in town set Igor up with a piano. Unfortunately, the piano was not only out of tune, but it was kept in a combination lumber-storage room and chicken coop! Igor was happy to be alone, though, and he started working on what would be some of his best-loved pieces, including *The Soldier's Tale* and *The Wedding*.

An illustration of some costume designs for the first production of *The Wedding*

To make some extra money, Igor began conducting and playing the piano in public for the first time. He was so nervous he sometimes forgot parts of his own music. Once he froze up when he noticed the reflection of his fingers in the polished wood of the piano!

Soon after World War I ended, Igor Stravinsky surprised everyone by changing his style completely. Instead of writing modern-sounding music based on Russian stories and folk tunes, Igor began composing pieces that were more like the classical music written centuries earlier by Mozart, Haydn, and Bach. Igor's *Pulcinella,* Symphony in Three Movements, and Symphony in C were inspired by composers from the past, but Igor added his own touches to create a very beautiful and new classical style of music.

A sketch of Stravinsky bowing to an appreciative audience after he has just finished conducting one of his pieces

Music from Stravinsky's *Rite of Spring* was used in the Disney movie *Fantasia* (above).

Igor Stravinsky thought it was very important to keep trying new things. For a while he experimented with jazz. He even did a ballet for the circus. The dancers in *Circus Polka,* however, weren't ballerinas—they were elephants! Igor's music was also used in Walt Disney's animated movie *Fantasia*. Walt Disney thought the savage rhythms of *The Rite of Spring* would be perfect for the part about the beginning of the world.

Igor Stravinsky became friends with many famous artists throughout his life, including Henri Matisse and Pablo Picasso. These artists designed sets and costumes and posters for many of Stravinsky's ballets.

A sketch of world-famous artist Pablo Picasso with Stravinsky

Igor Stravinsky, at the age of 76, conducting a rehearsal with the BBC Symphony Orchestra in London

Igor Stravinsky lived to be 88 years old. He composed music until he was 85. Igor spent the last few years of his life listening to and enjoying the music of other great composers.

With his startling new rhythmic sounds, Igor Stravinsky, maybe more than any other composer, led music into the 20th century and modern times.

It's pretty easy to find Stravinsky's music on classical radio stations. You can also borrow tapes and compact discs at many libraries.